PIANO
VOCAL
GUITAR

Hillsong LIVE

A BEAUTIFUL EXCHANGE

ISBN 978-1-61774-093-0

HAL•LEONARD®
CORPORATION
7777 W. BLUEMOUND RD. P.O. BOX 13819 MILWAUKEE, WI 53213

Visit Hal Leonard Online at
www.halleonard.com

Our God Is Love

Words and Music by JOEL HOUSTON
and SCOTT LIGERTWOOD

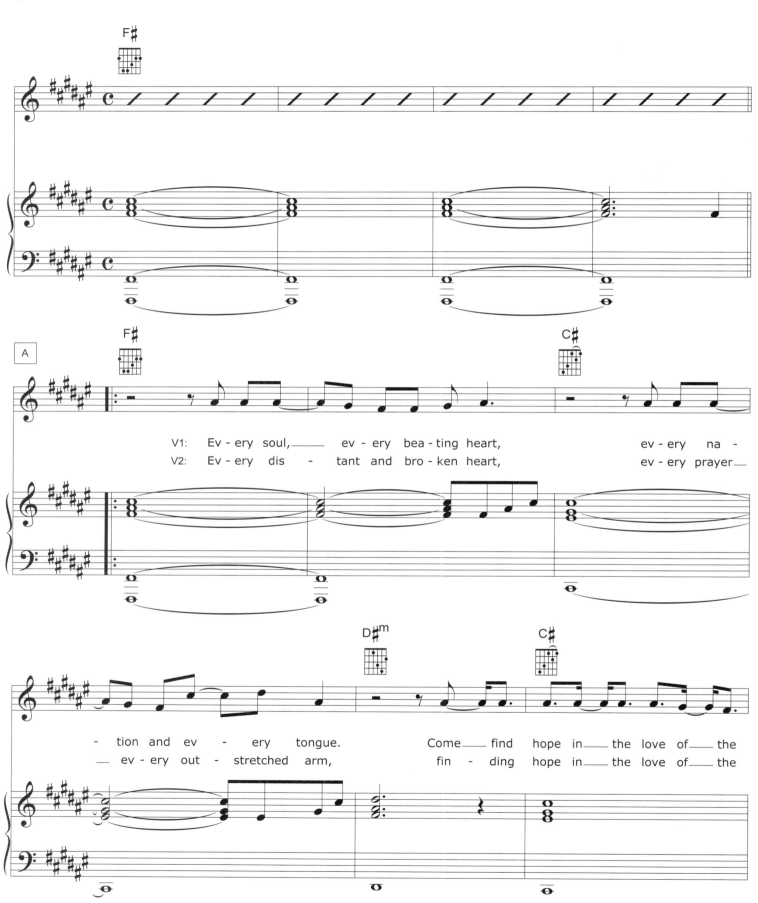

V1: Ev - ery soul,___ ev - ery bea - ting heart, ___ ev - ery na -
V2: Ev - ery dis - tant and bro - ken heart, ___ ev - ery prayer___

- tion and ev - ery tongue. Come___ find hope in___ the love of___ the
___ ev - ery out - stretched arm, fin - ding hope in___ the love of___ the

CCLI: 5636866

6

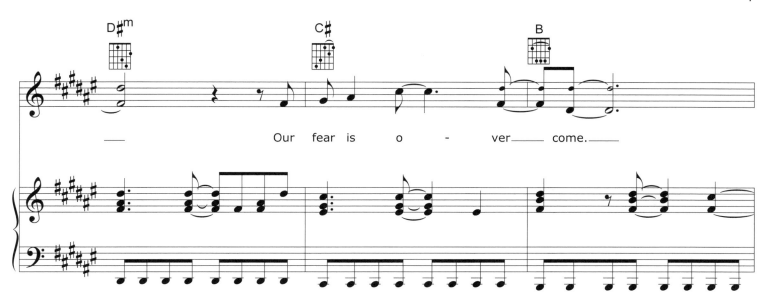

Our fear is o - ver___ come.___

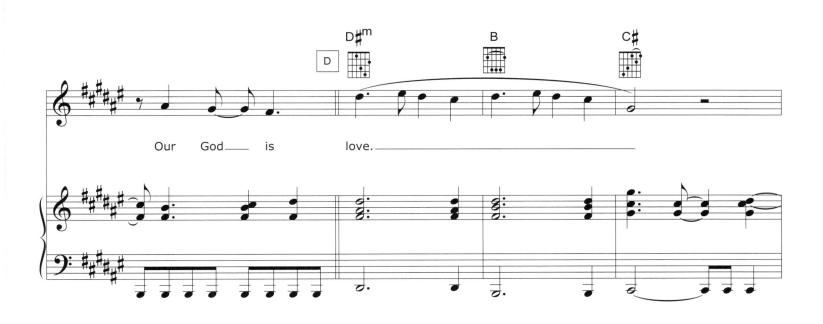

Our God___ is love.___

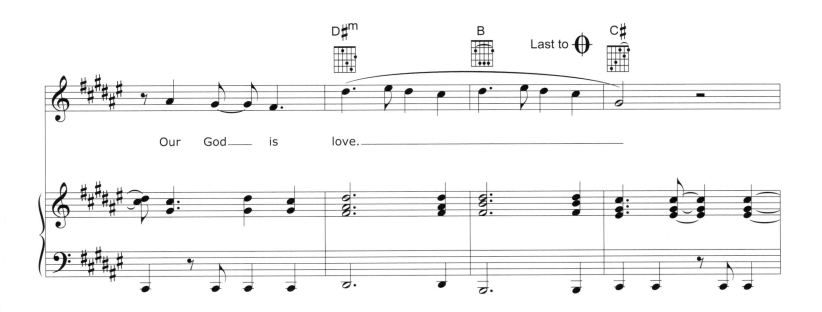

Our God___ is love.___

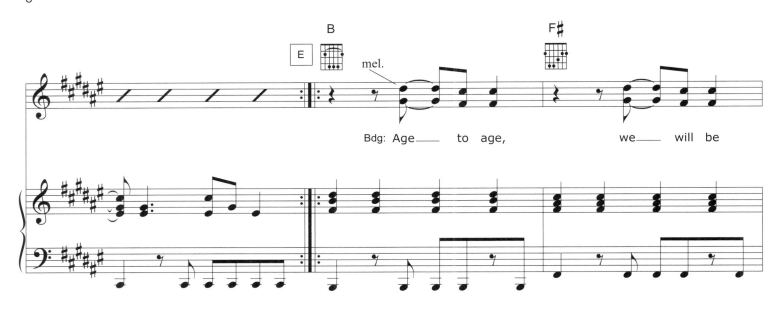

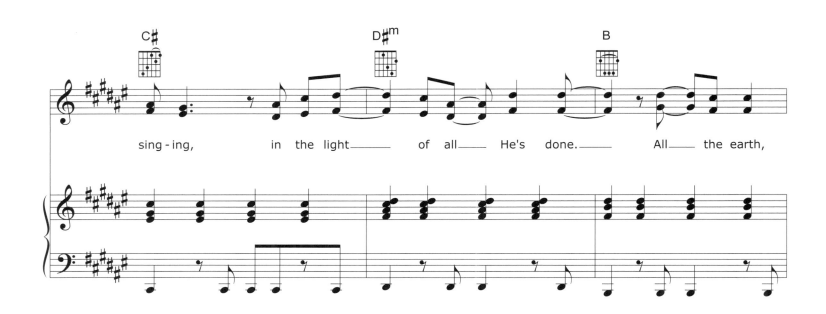

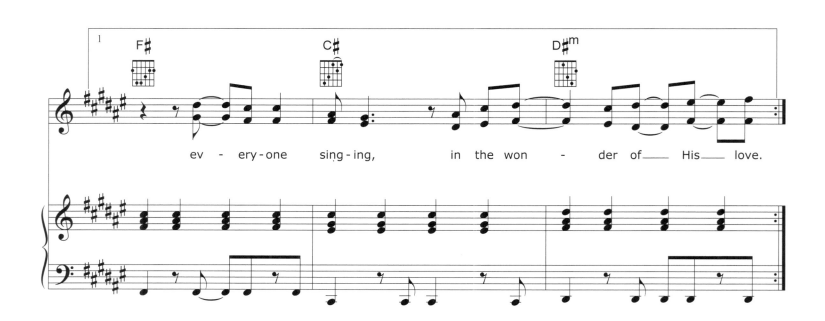

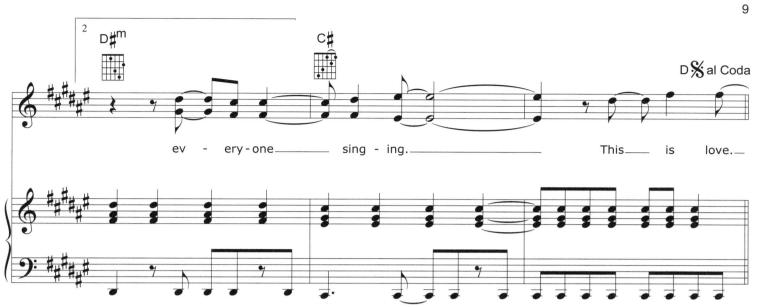

ev - ery-one_____ sing - ing._____ This___ is love.___

___ Our God___ is love._____

Our God___ is love._____

Open My Eyes

Words and Music by REUBEN MORGAN
and BRADEN LANG

CCLI: 5636873

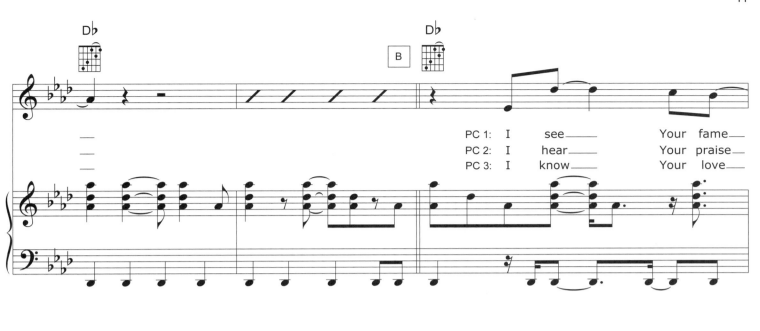

PC 1: I see____ Your fame____
PC 2: I hear____ Your praise____
PC 3: I know____ Your love____

____ in all____ of the earth.____ And I_____
____ in all____ of the earth.____ And I_____
____ is all____ that I need.____ And I_____

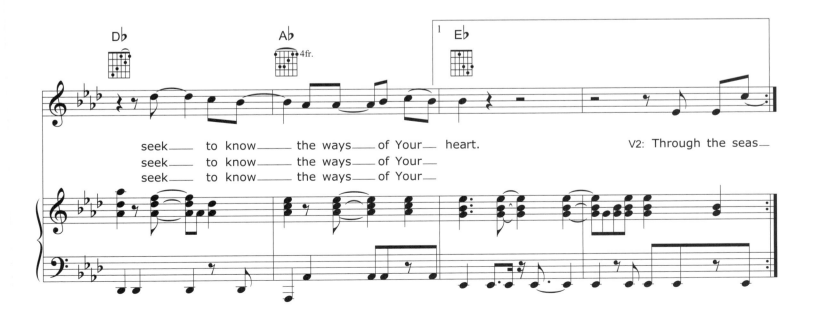

seek____ to know____ the ways____ of Your____ heart.
seek____ to know____ the ways____ of Your____
seek____ to know____ the ways____ of Your____

V2: Through the seas____

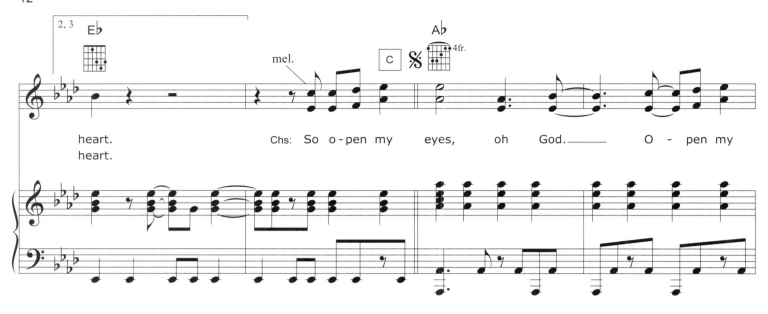

heart.
heart.

Chs: So o-pen my eyes, oh God._____ O - pen my

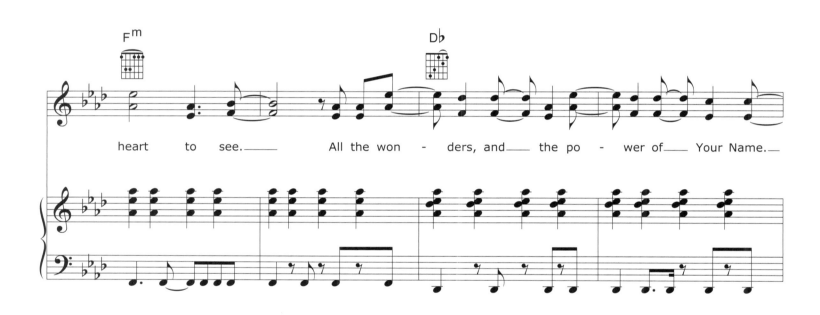

heart to see._____ All the won - ders, and___ the po - wer of___ Your Name.___

___ By Your grace, I'll live._____ By Your

PC 3: I know___ Your love___ is all___ that I need.___ And I,___

seek___ to know___ the ways___ of Your___ heart.

heart.

So o - pen my

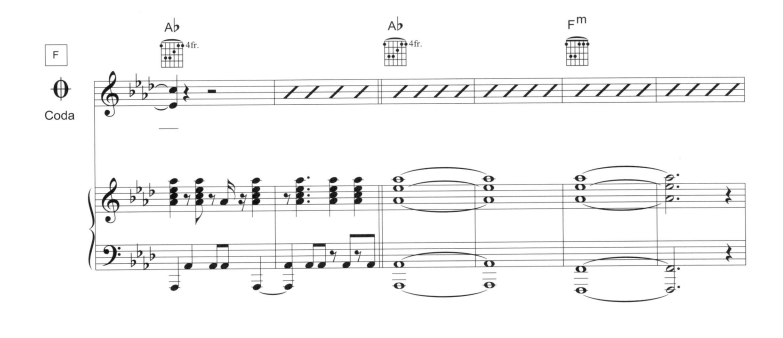

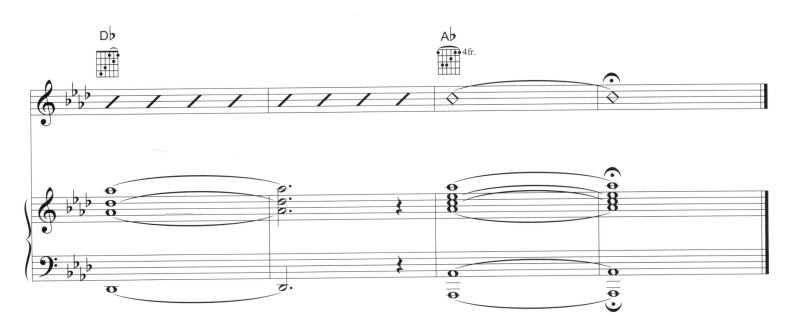

Forever Reign

Words and Music by REUBEN MORGAN
and JASON INGRAM

hope, You are hope, You have co - vered all my sin._____ V2: You are
life, You are life, in You death has lost its sting._____
God, You are God, of all else I'm let - ting go._____

C1: Oh, I'm run - ning to Your

arms, I'm run - ning to Your arms. The ri - ches of Your

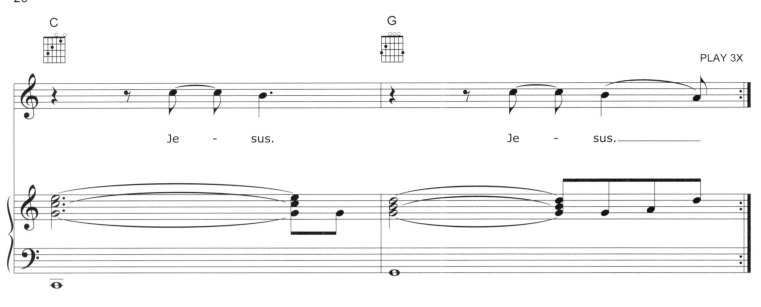

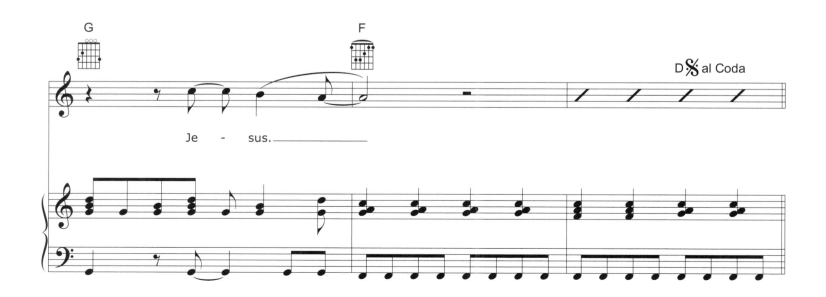

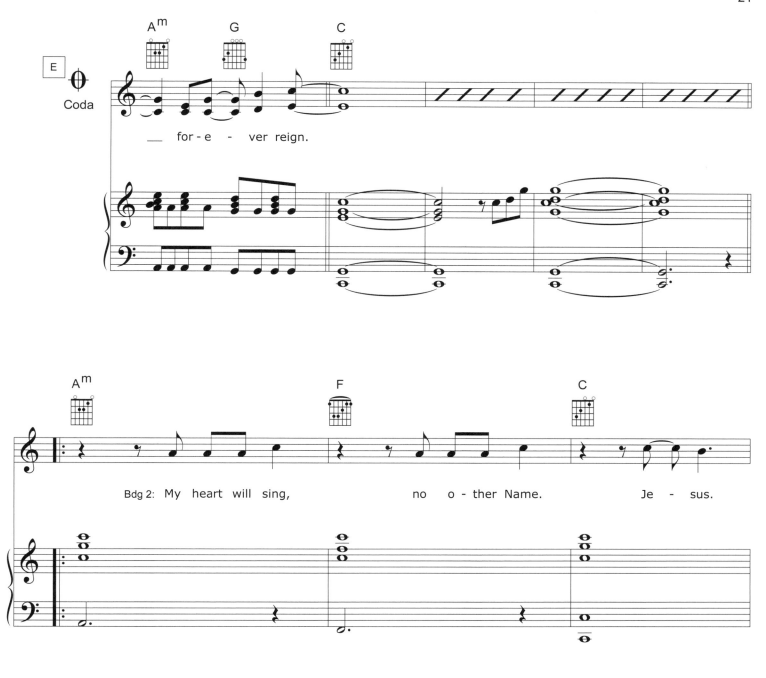

for - e - ver reign.

Bdg 2: My heart will sing, no o - ther Name. Je - sus.

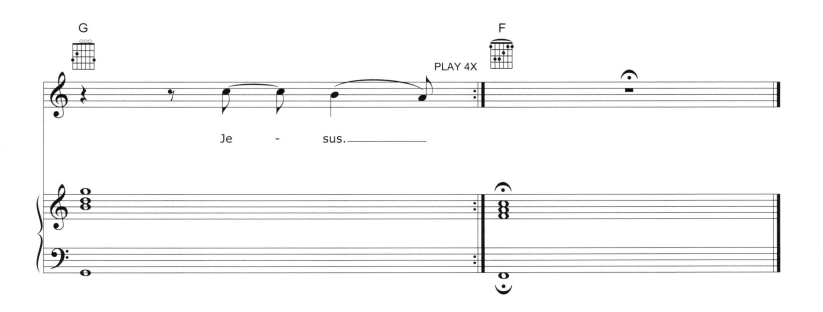

Je - sus.

The One Who Saves

Words and Music by
BEN FIELDING

V1: Come join the song. Lift your_____ voice,_____ as hea - ven and earth give_____

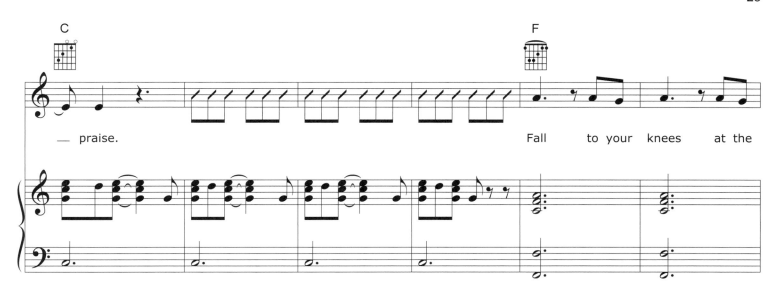

praise.   Fall   to your knees   at the

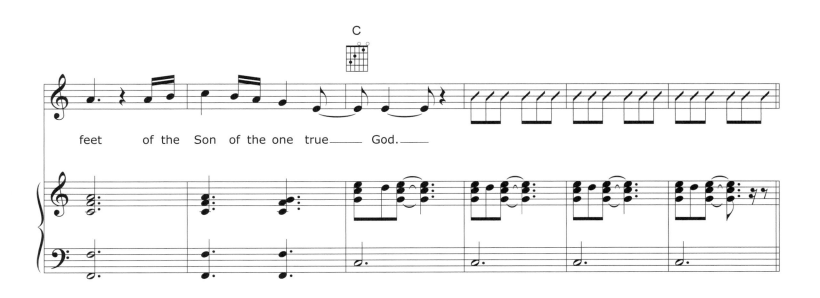

feet   of the Son of the one true___ God.___

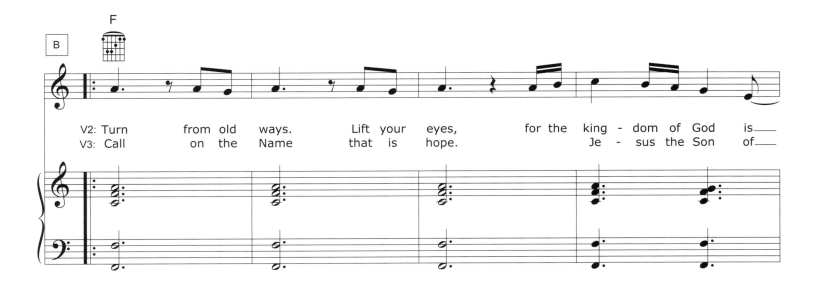

V2: Turn   from old   ways.   Lift your   eyes,   for the king - dom of God   is___
V3: Call   on the Name   that is hope.   Je - sus the Son   of___

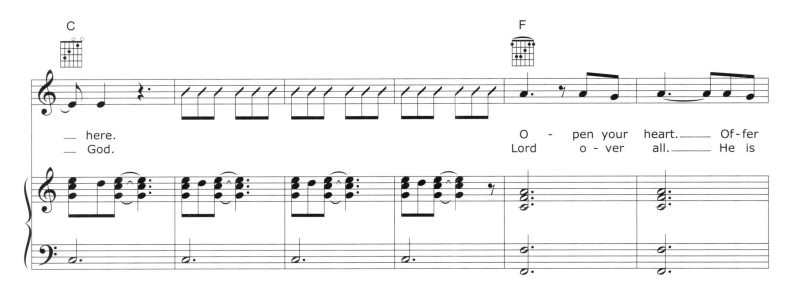

here.
God.
O - pen your heart.____ Of-fer
Lord o - ver all.____ He is

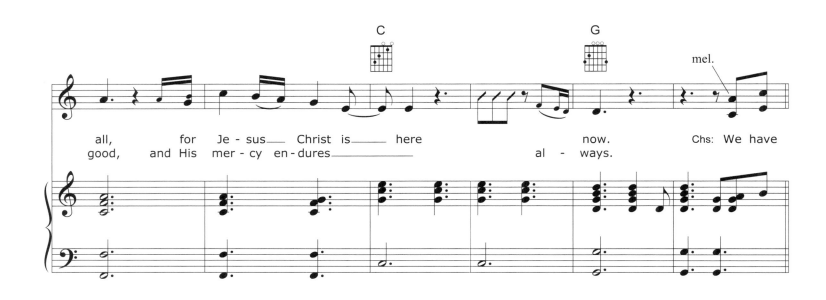

all, for Je - sus___ Christ is___ here now. Chs: We have
good, and His mer - cy en - dures___ al - ways.

found our hope. We have found our peace. We have found our rest in the

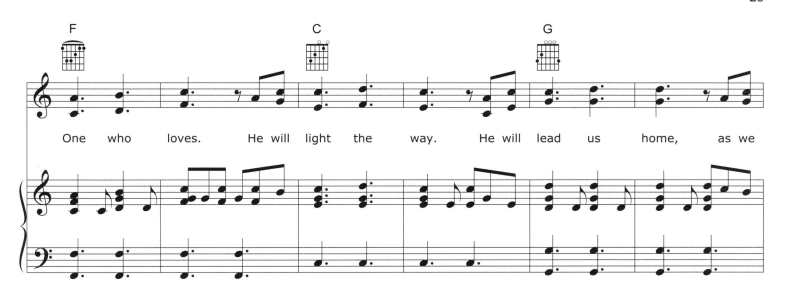

One who loves. He will light the way. He will lead us home, as we

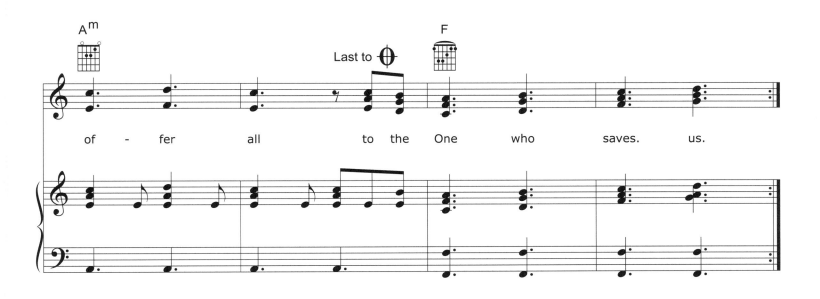

of - fer all to the One who saves. us.

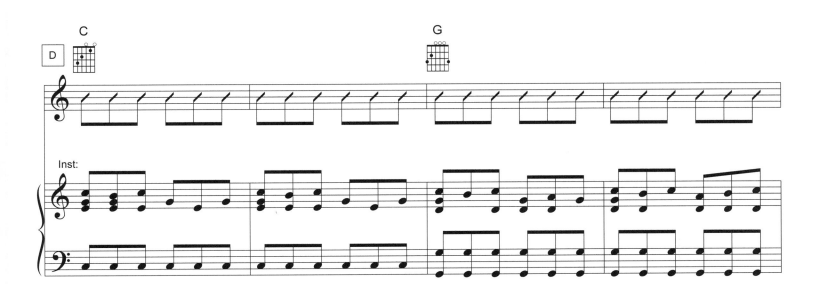

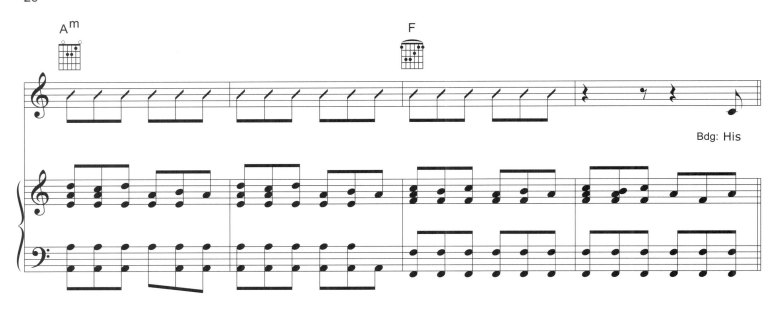

Bdg: His

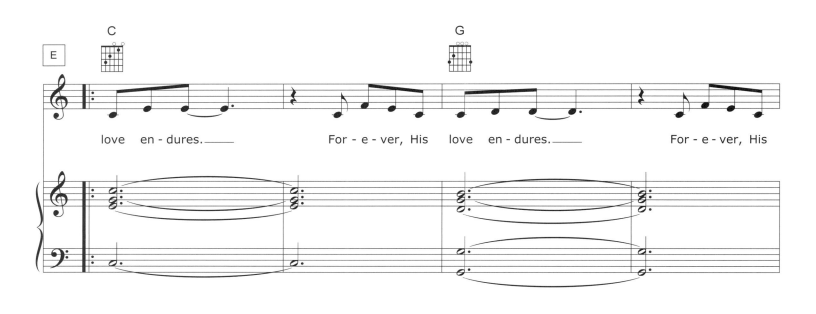

love en-dures._____ For-e-ver, His love en-dures._____ For-e-ver, His

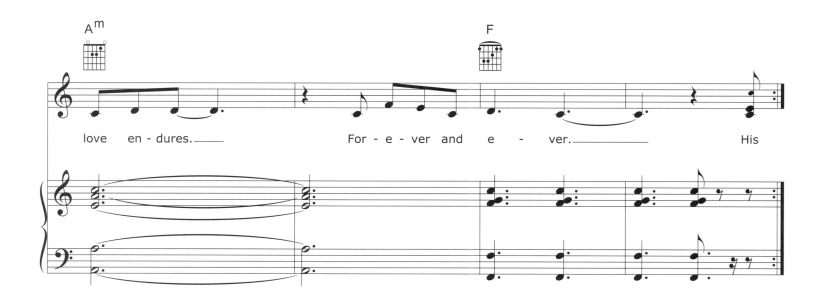

love en-dures._____ For-e-ver and e-ver._____ His

love en - dures._____ For - e - ver, His love en - dures._____

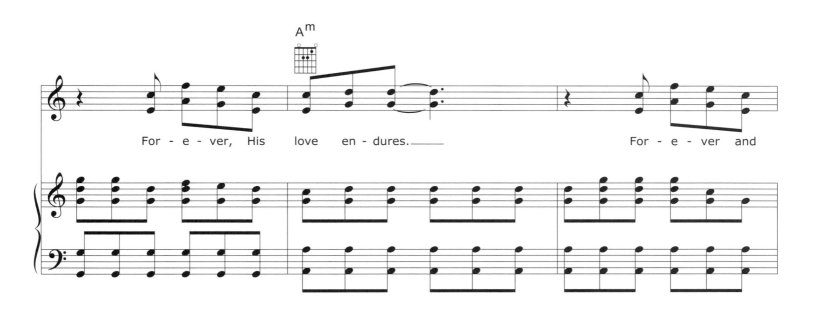

For - e - ver, His love en - dures._____ For - e - ver and

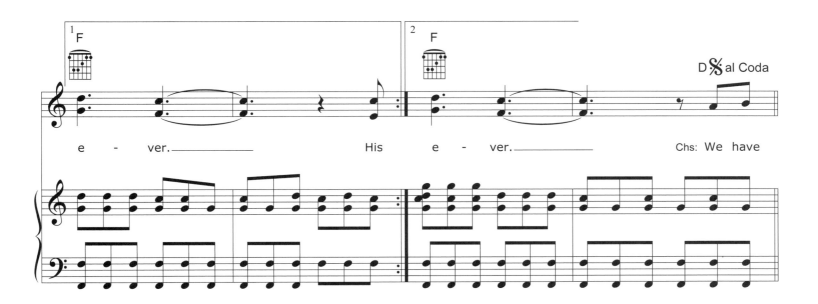

e - ver._____ His e - ver._____ Chs: We have

28

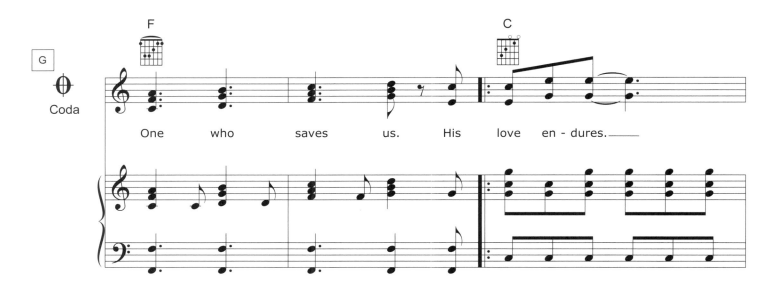

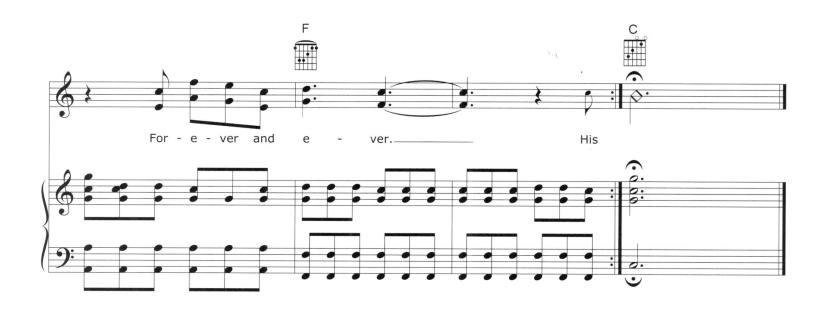

Like Incense / Sometimes By Step

LIKE INCENSE
Words and Music by
BROOKE LIGERTWOOD

V1: May my prayer like in - cense rise be - fore You. The
(v2:) all cre - a - tion I can see a li - mit. But

CCLI: 5637528

lif - ting of___ my hands___ a sa - cri - fice.___
Your com - mands___ are bound - less and___ have none.___ So

Oh, Lord Je - sus, turn Your eyes___ u - pon___ me, for
Your word is my joy and me - di - ta - tion. From the

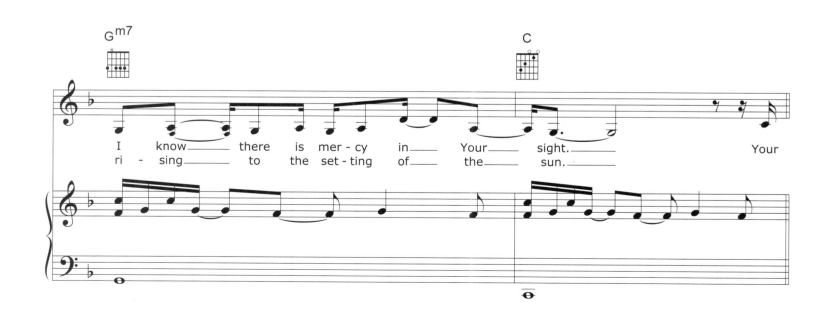

I know___ there is mer - cy in___ Your___ sight.___ Your
ri - sing___ to the set - ting of___ the___ sun.

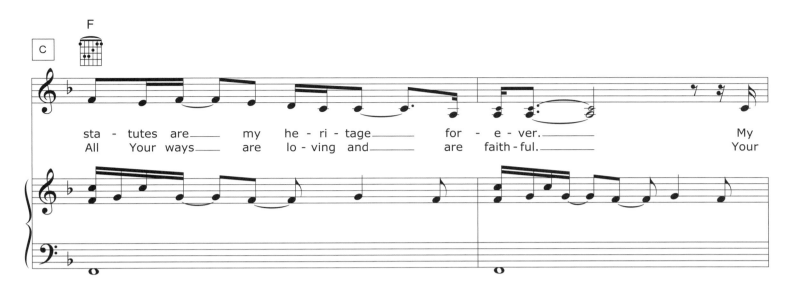

C | F

sta - tutes are___ my he - ri - tage___ for - e - ver.___ My
All Your ways___ are lo - ving and___ are faith - ful.___ Your

Dm

heart is set___ on kee - ping Your___ de - crees.___ Please
road is nar - row, but Your bur - den light.___ Be -

B♭

still my an - xious urge___ to - ward___ re - bel - lion.___
cause You glad - ly lean___ to lead___ the hum - ble.

SOMETIMES BY STEP
Words and Music by
DAVID "BEAKER" STRASSER

34

C3: Oh

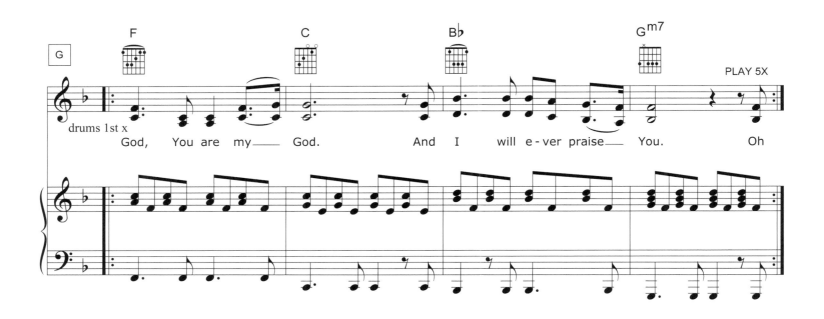

drums 1st x

God, You are my___ God. And I will e-ver praise___ You. Oh

God, You are my___ God. And I will e-ver praise___ You. Tag: I will

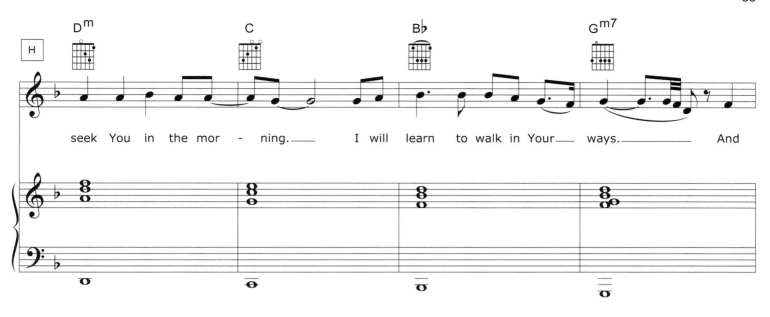

seek You in the mor - ning.___ I will learn to walk in Your___ ways._____ And

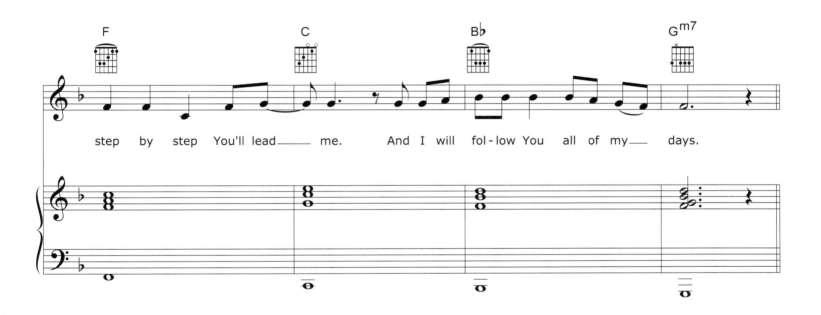

step by step You'll lead___ me. And I will fol-low You all of my___ days.

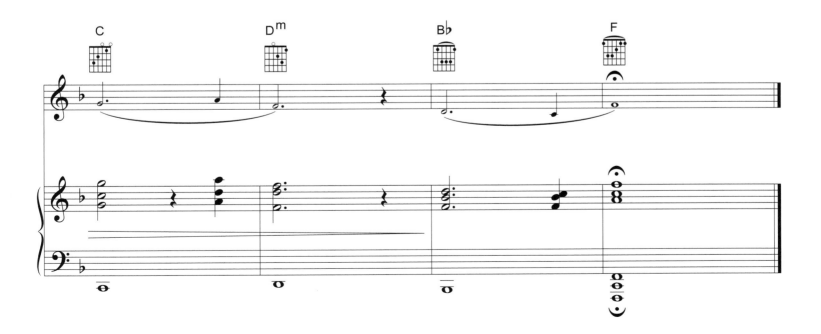

The Greatness Of Our God

Words and Music by REUBEN MORGAN, JASON INGRAM
and STUART GARRARD

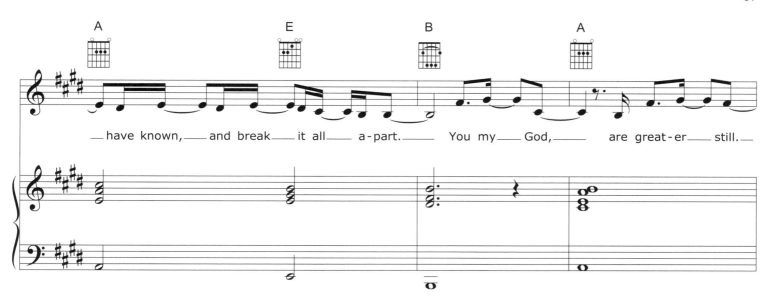

have known,— and break— it all— a-part.— You my— God,— are great-er— still.—

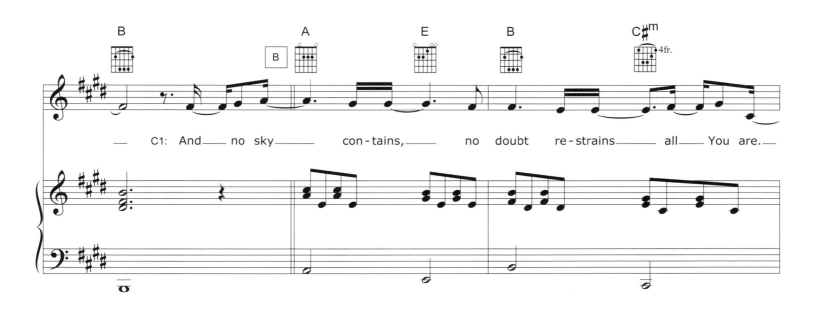

— C1: And— no sky— con-tains,— no doubt re-strains— all— You are.—

— The great-ness of our God. I spend my life to know,— and I'm—

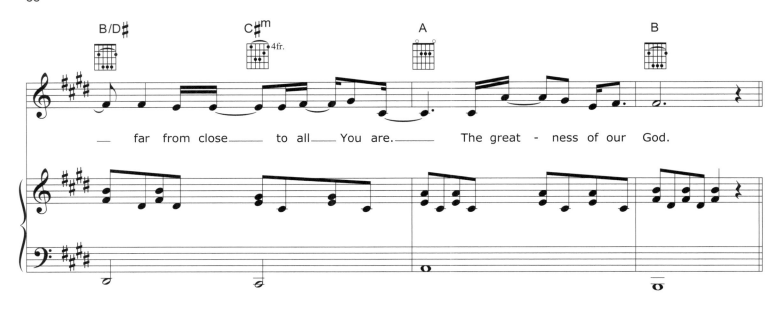

far from close ___ to all ___ You are. ___ The great - ness of our God.

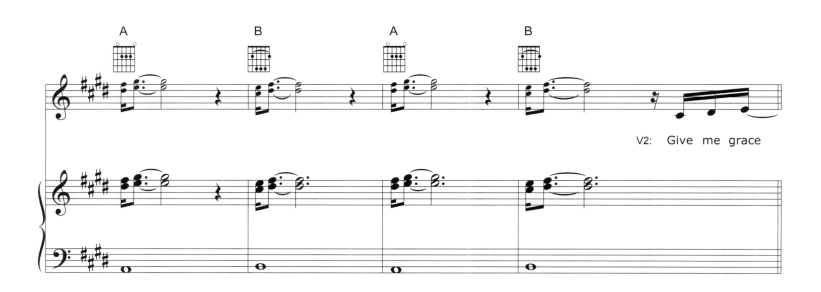

V2: Give me grace

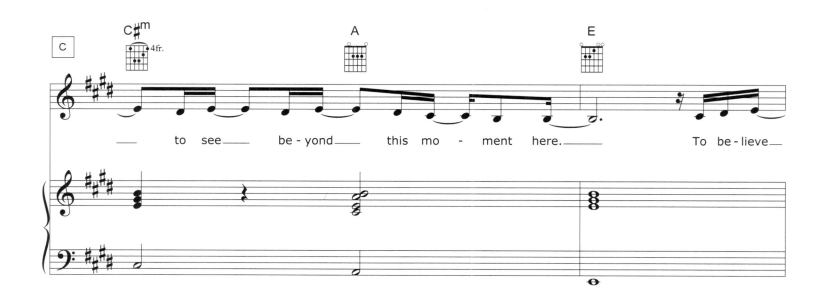

to see ___ be - yond ___ this mo - ment here. ___ To be - lieve ___

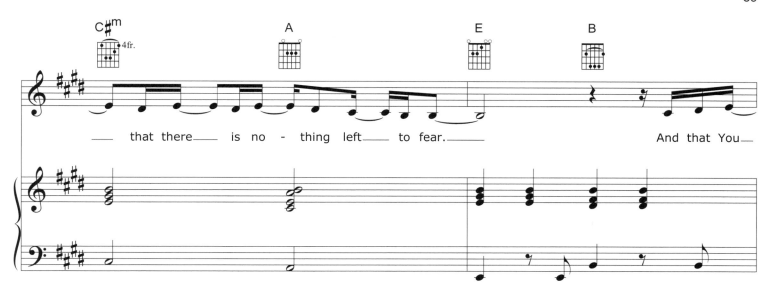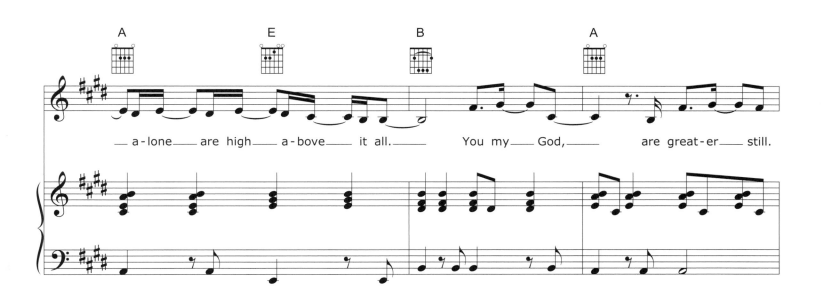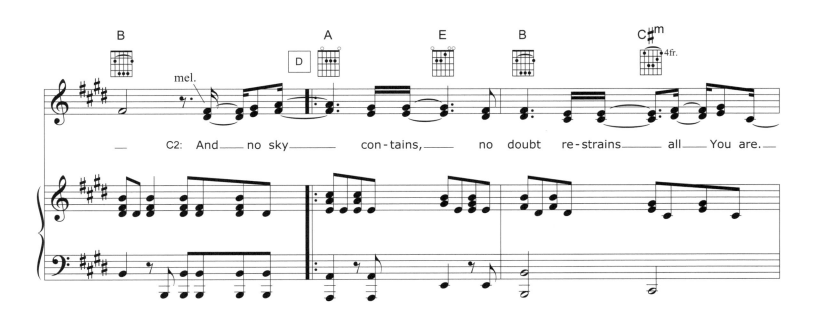

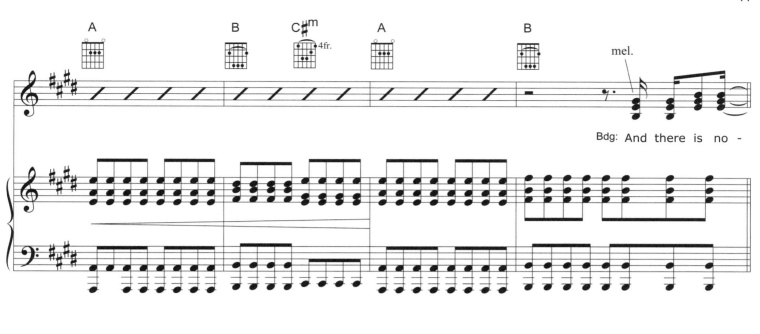

Bdg: And there is no -

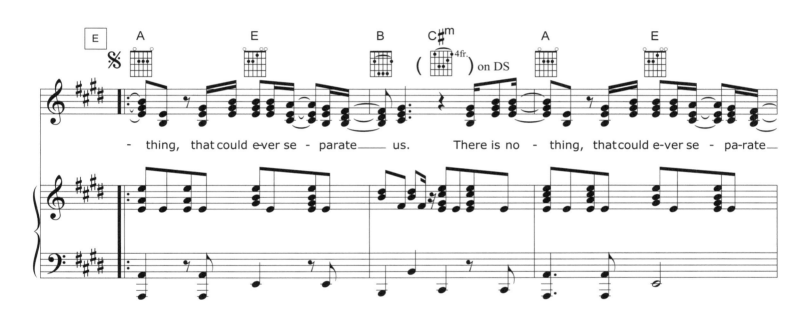

- thing, that could ever se - parate us. There is no - thing, that could e-ver se - pa-rate

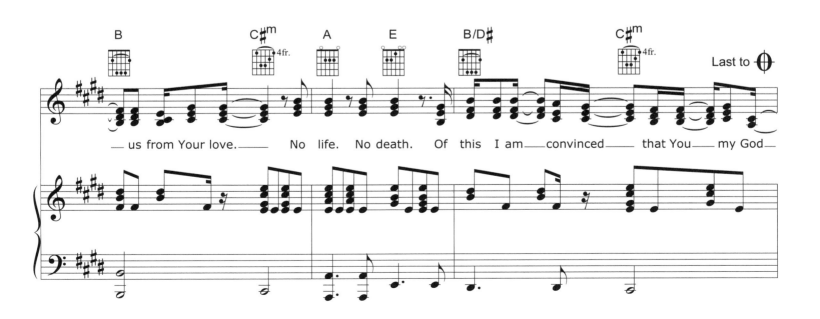

us from Your love. No life. No death. Of this I am convinced that You my God

42

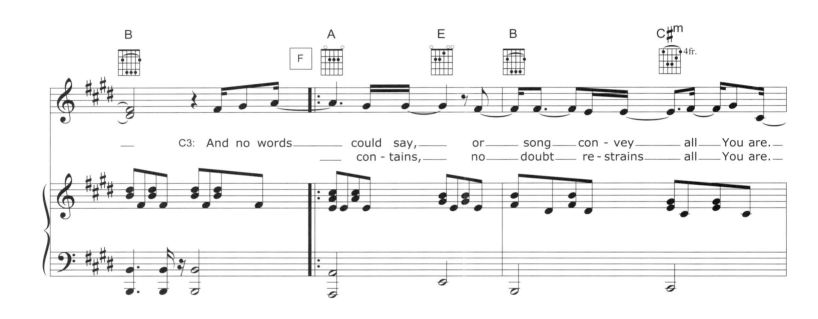

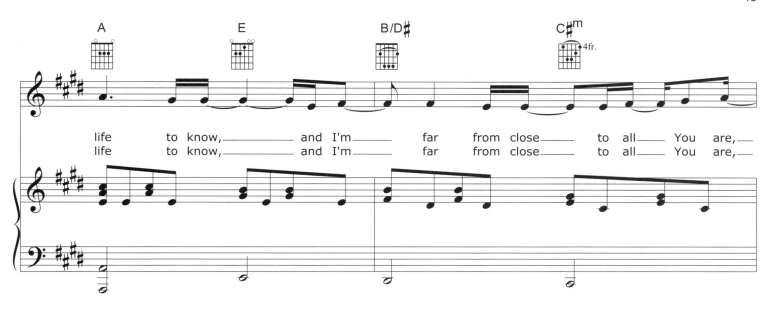

life to know,_____ and I'm_____ far from close_____ to all____ You are,

1.

____ the great - ness of our God. And no sky____

2.

____ the great - ness of our God. All____ You are,____

the great - ness of our God.

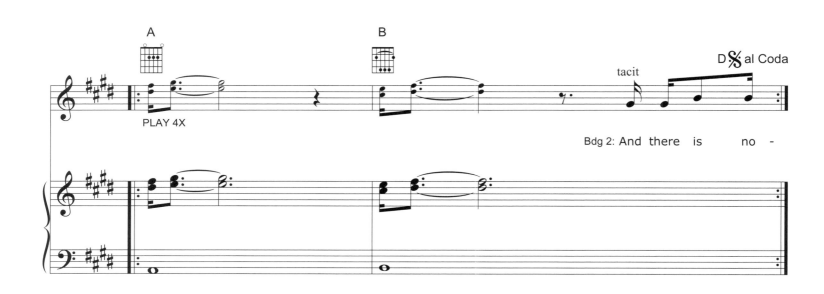

PLAY 4X

tacit

D.S. al Coda

Bdg 2: And there is no -

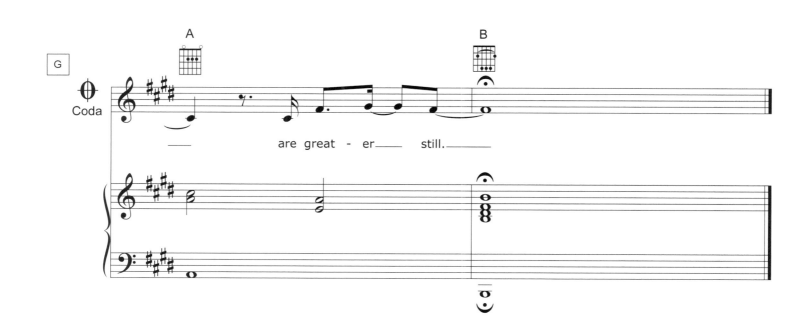

Coda

are great - er____ still.____

The Father's Heart

Words and Music by GIO GALANTI
and JORIM KELLY

♩ = 123

V1: When the walls___ close in___ a-round___ me.___ Let Your glo -
V2: Upon the throne___ of sweet___ sur - ren ___ - der,___ I have no -
V3: Hum - ble King,___ You go___ be - fore___ me.___ By Your grace,

CCLI: 5636907

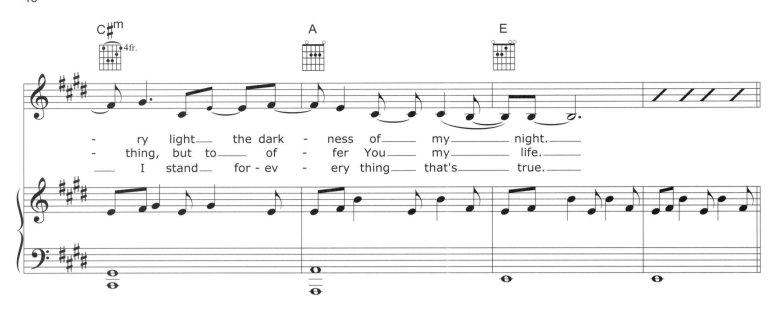

-ry light___ the dark - ness of___ my___ night.___
-thing, but to___ of - fer You___ my___ life.___
___ I stand___ for - ev - ery thing___ that's___ true.___

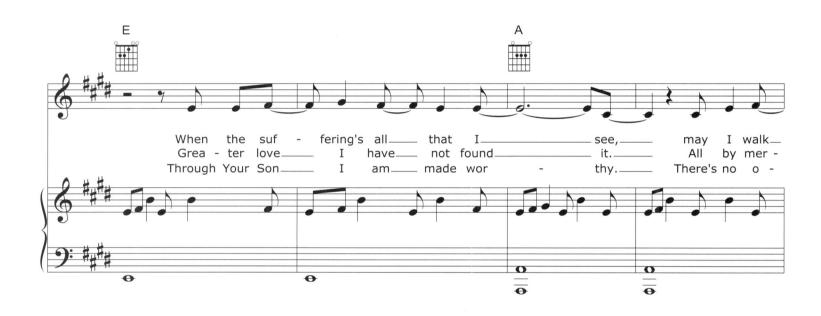

When the suf - fering's all___ that I___ see,___ may I walk___
Grea - ter love___ I have___ not found___ it.___ All by mer -
Through Your Son___ I am___ made wor - thy.___ There's no o -

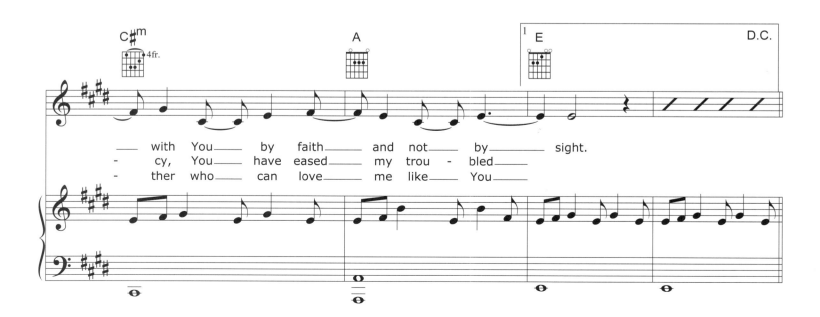

___ with You___ by faith___ and not___ by___ sight.
-cy, You___ have eased___ my trou - bled___
-ther who___ can love___ me like___ You___

mind. O - pen hear - ted, I will search and I will
do. And for - e - ver I'll keep run - ning back to

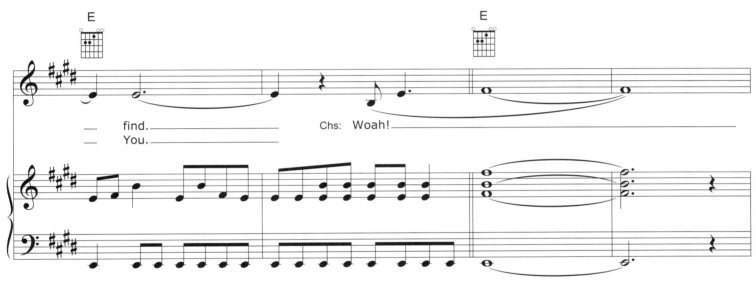

find. Chs: Woah!
You.

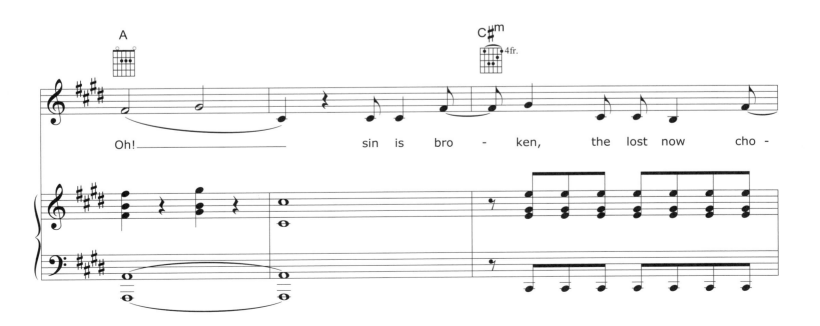

Oh! sin is bro - ken, the lost now cho -

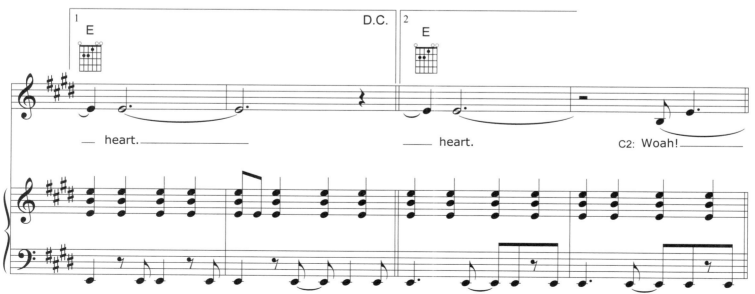

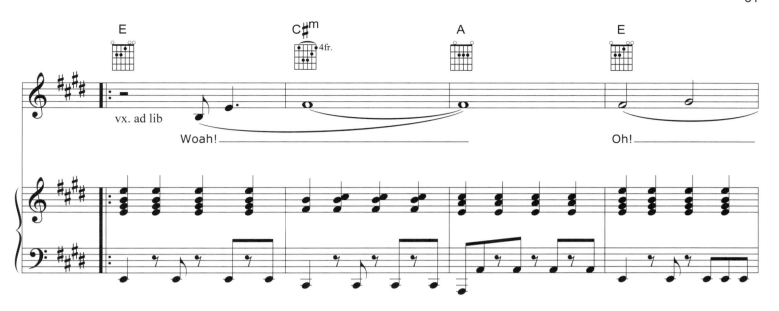

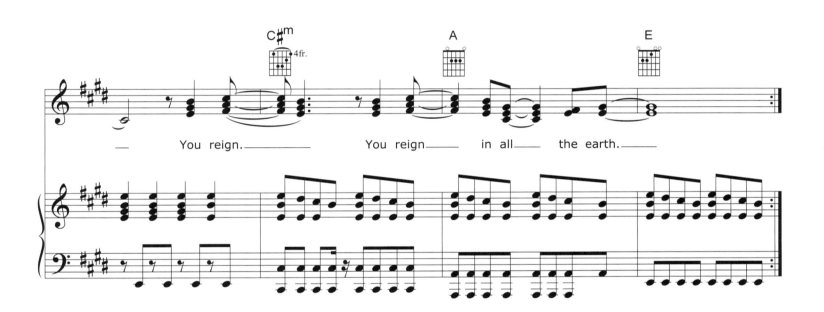

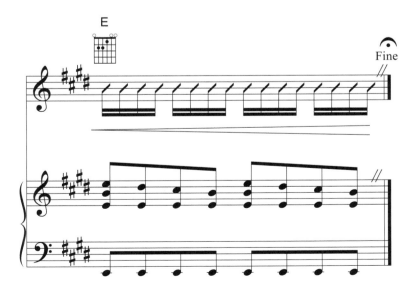

You

Words and Music by
JOEL HOUSTON

CCLI: 5636914

V2: My heart

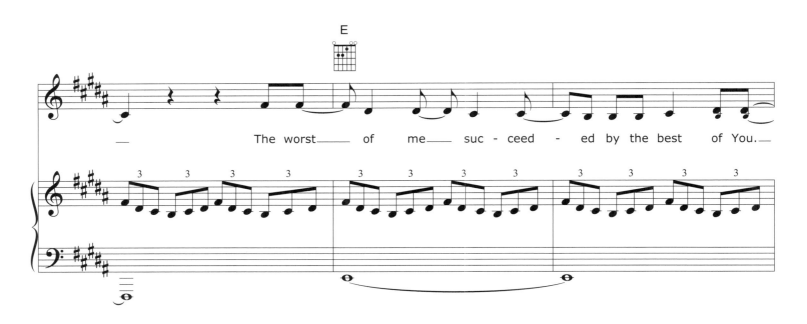

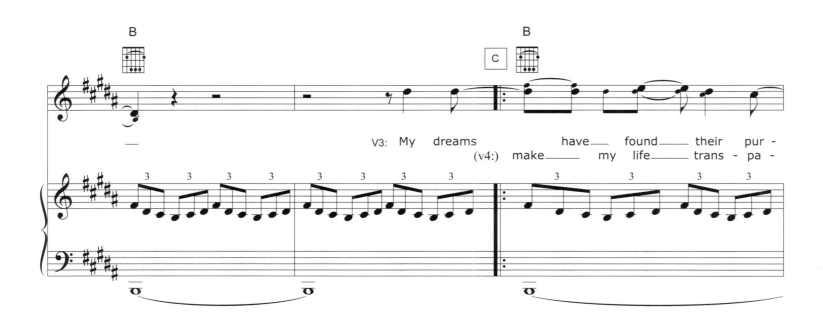

- pose,____ my fu - ture__ in__ Your__ hands.____ This life____
- rent,____ Your life__ in__ mine__ dis - played. And let ev -

____ would have__ no mea - ning if it weren't for You.____
- ery earth - ly glo - ry go__ back to You.____

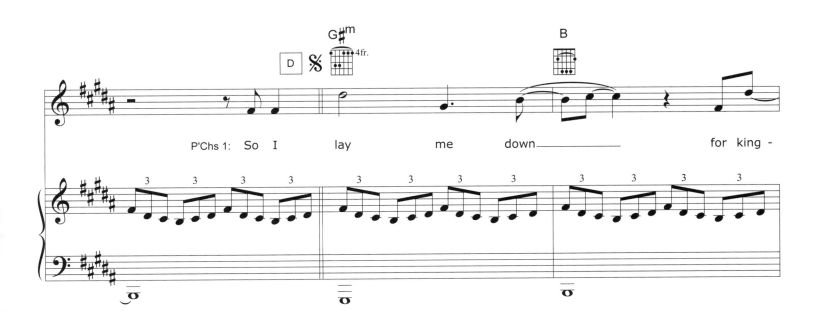

P'Chs 1: So I lay me down____ for king -

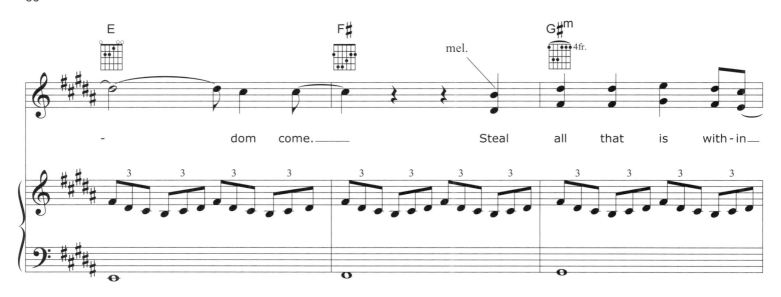

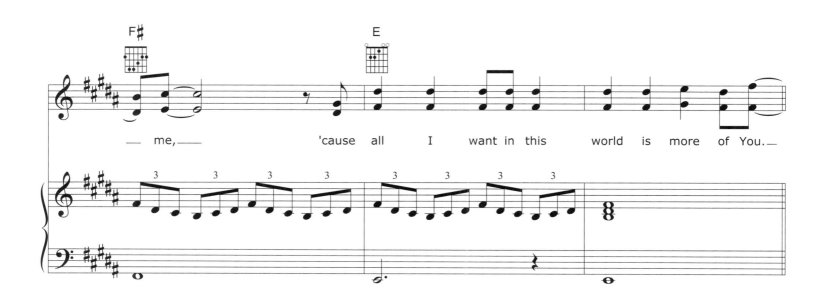

fade a - way,___ Your___ light___ for all the world to see.___

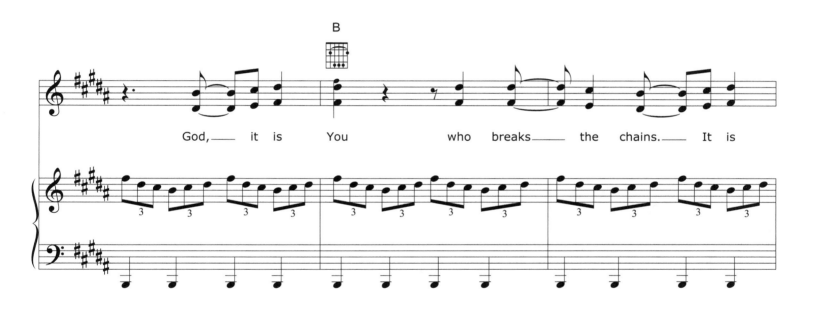

God,___ it is You who breaks___ the chains.___ It is

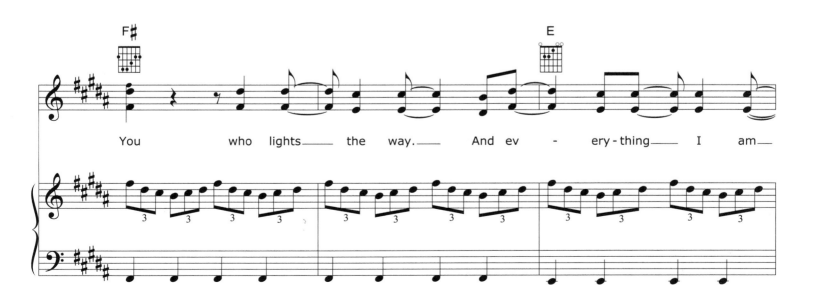

You who lights___ the way.___ And ev - ery-thing___ I am___

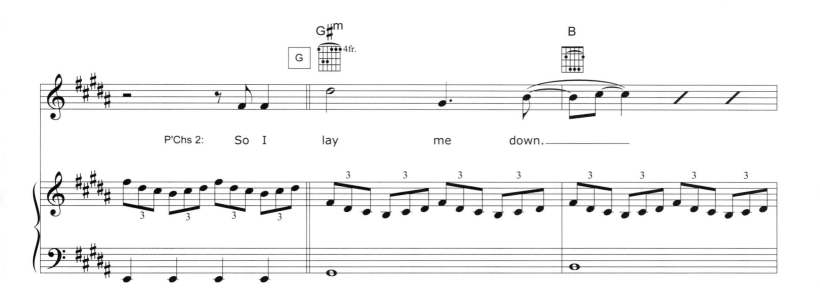

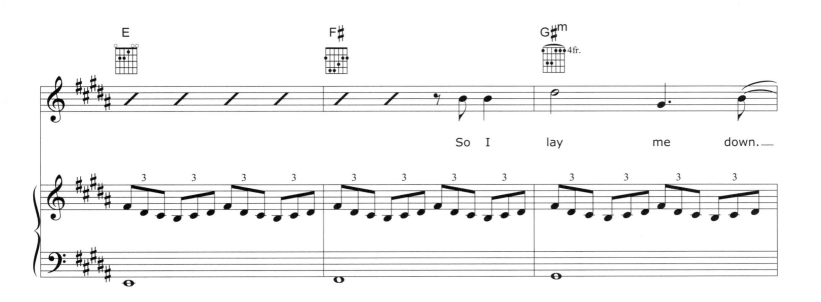

Love Like Fire

Words and Music by
MATT CROCKER

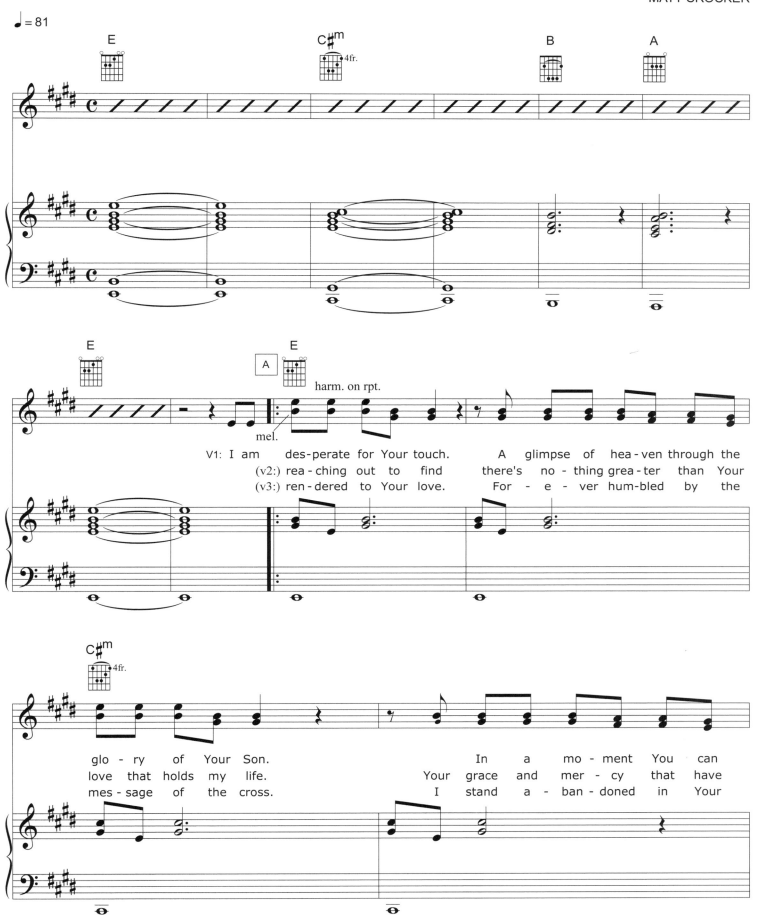

V1: I am des-per-ate for Your touch. A glimpse of hea-ven through the
(v2:) rea-ching out to find there's no-thing grea-ter than Your
(v3:) ren-dered to Your love. For - e - ver hum-bled by the

glo - ry of Your Son. In a mo - ment You can
love that holds my life. Your grace and mer - cy that have
mes - sage of the cross. I stand a - ban - doned in Your

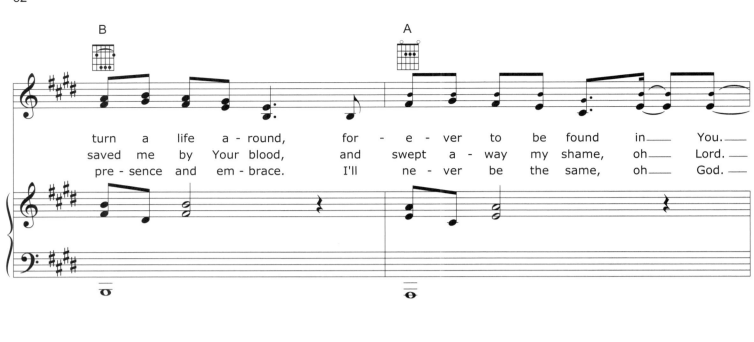

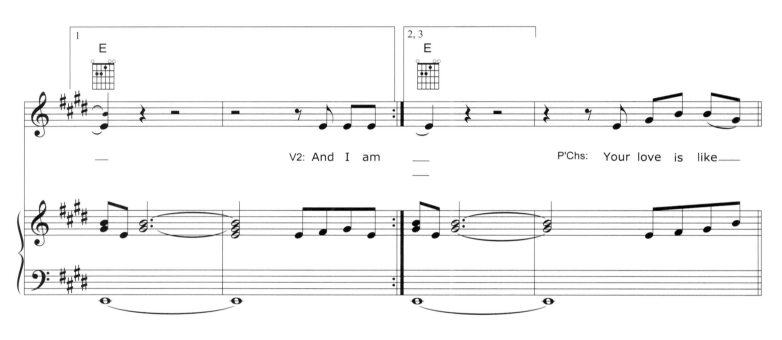

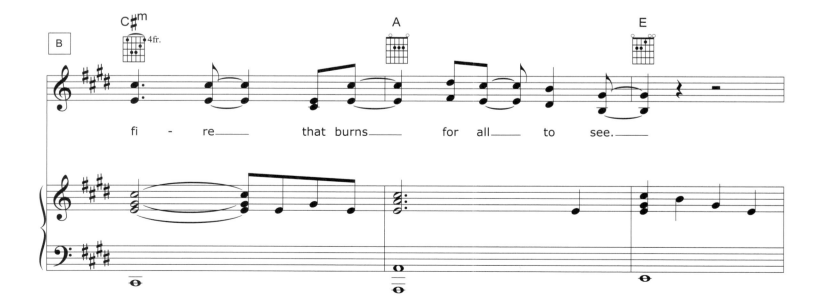

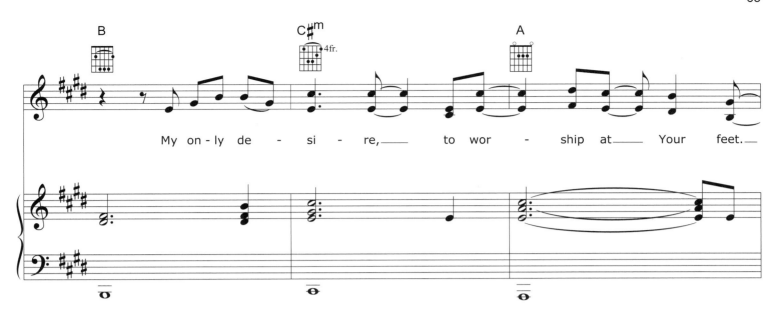

My on-ly de - si - re,___ to wor - ship at___ Your feet.___

___ So let this___ fire___ con-sume___ my life.___ Chs: Let Your love___ take me dee - per.

Draw me clo - ser to where___ You are.___ All I want___ is more___ of You.

64

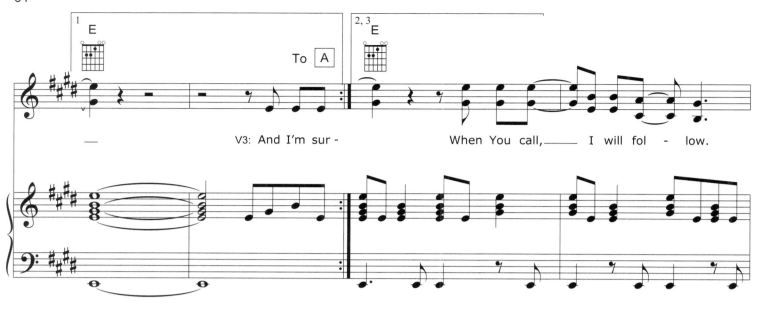

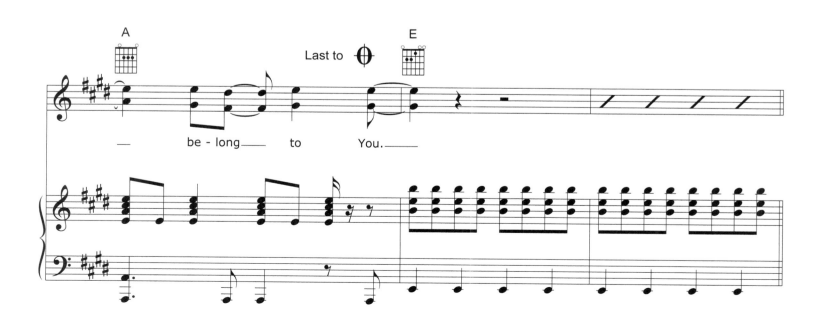

P'Chs 2: Your love is like____

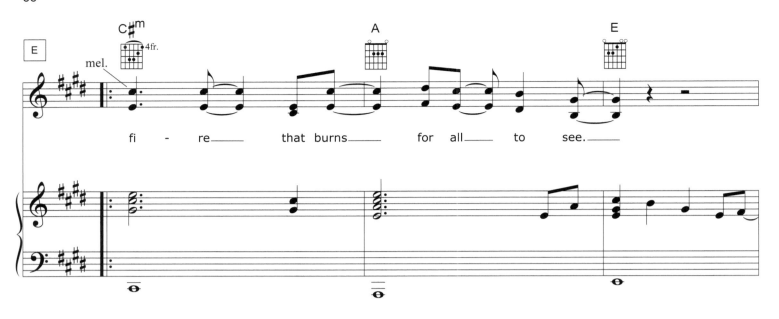

fi - re____ that burns____ for all____ to see.____

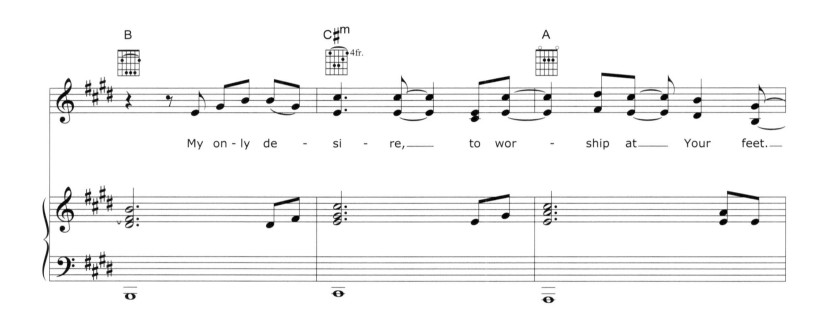

My on - ly de - si - re,____ to wor - ship at____ Your feet.

Your love is like____ ____ So let this____ fire con-sume____ my life.____

Believe

Words and Music by REUBEN MORGAN
and DARLENE ZSCHECH

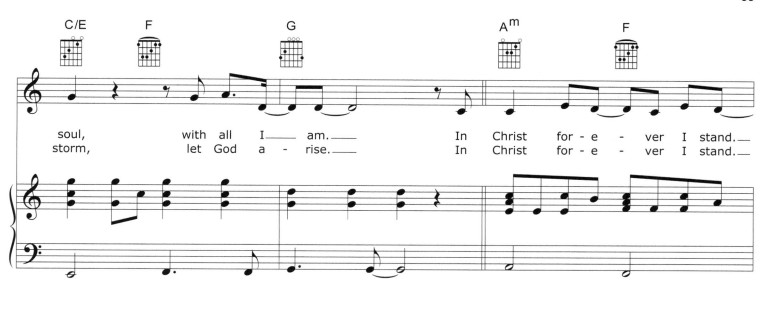

soul, with all I___ am.___ In Christ for - e - ver I stand.___
storm, let God a - rise.___ In Christ for - e - ver I stand.___

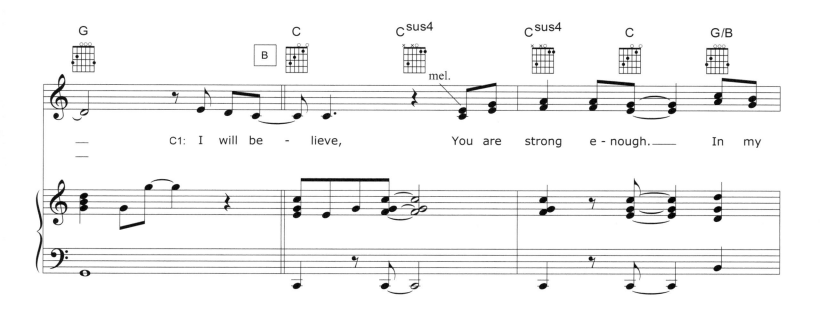

___ C1: I will be - lieve, You are strong e - nough.___ In my

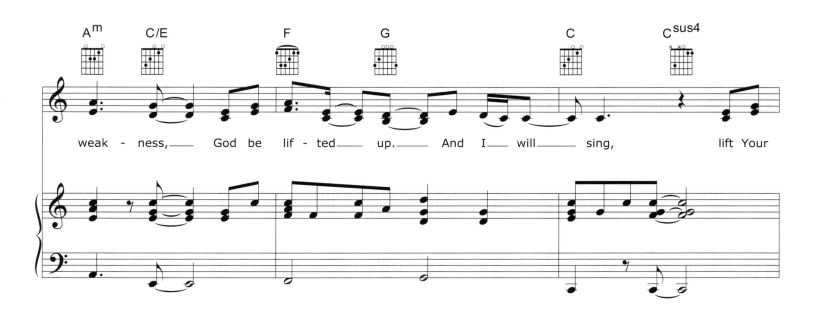

weak - ness,___ God be lif - ted___ up.___ And I___ will___ sing, lift Your

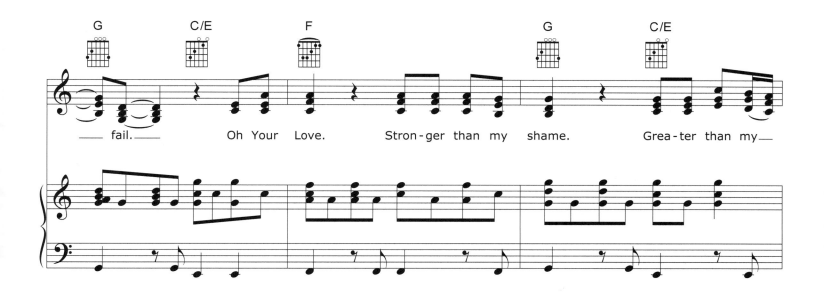

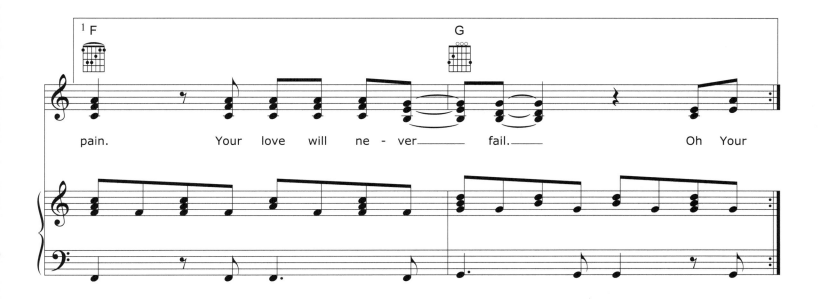

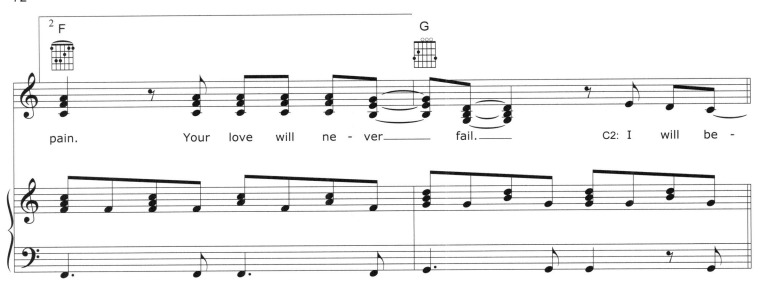

pain. Your love will ne - ver_____ fail._____ C2: I will be -

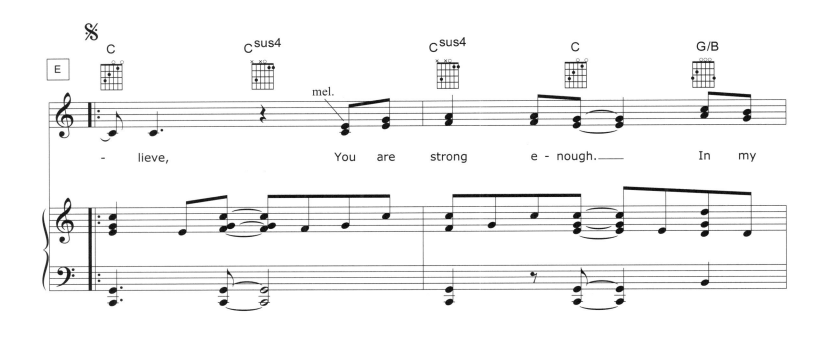

- lieve, You are strong e - nough._____ In my

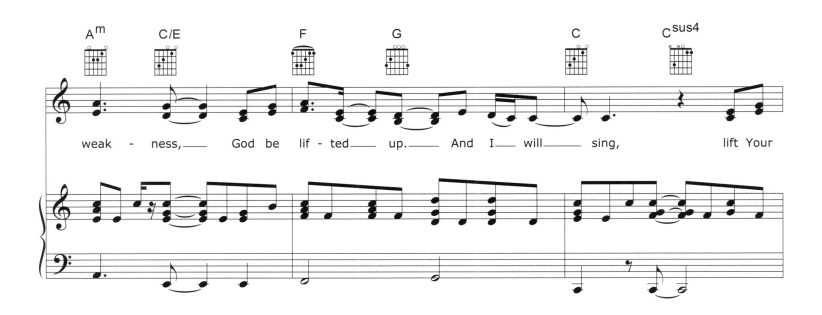

weak - ness,_____ God be lif - ted_____ up._____ And I will_____ sing, lift Your

Beautiful Exchange

Words and Music by
JOEL HOUSTON

CCLI: 5637470

- sioned, I was lost___ and in - se - cure.___ Still mer - cy___

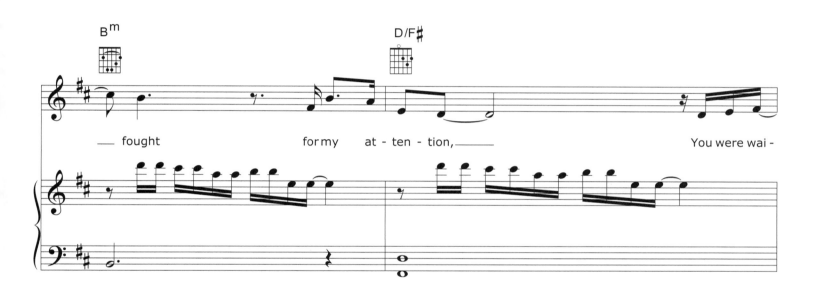

___ fought for my at - ten - tion,___ You were wai -

- ting at___ the door.___ Then I let You___

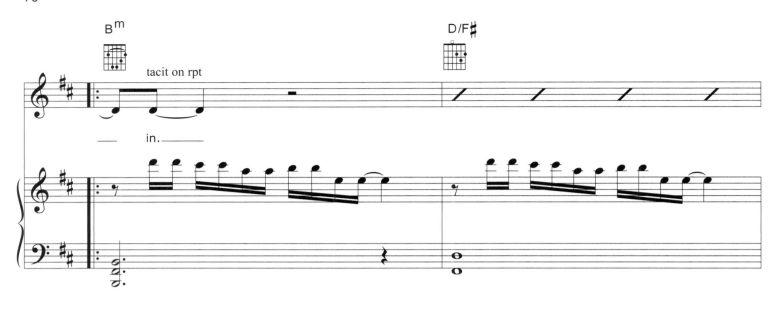

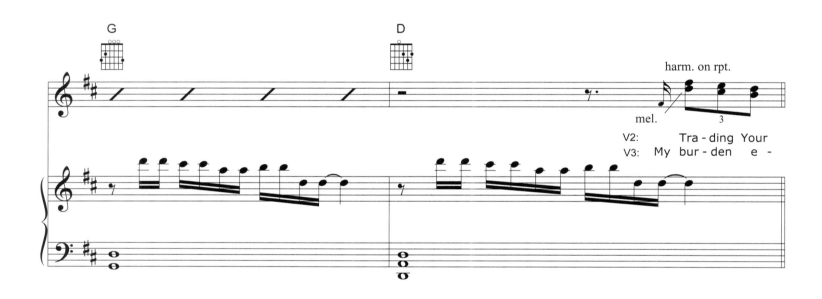

demp - tion,_____ You car - ried all___ the blame._____ Brea - king the
- thing___ that can take this love___ a - way.___ And my on - ly de-

curse of our con - di - tion,_____ per - fec -
sire and sole am - bi - tion,_____ is to love__

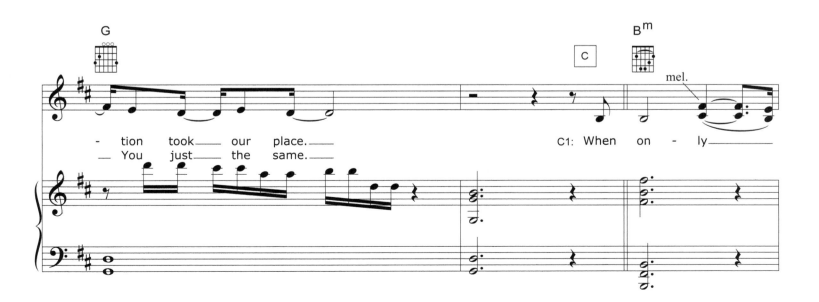

- tion took___ our place.___ C1: When on - ly_____
___ You just___ the same.___

78

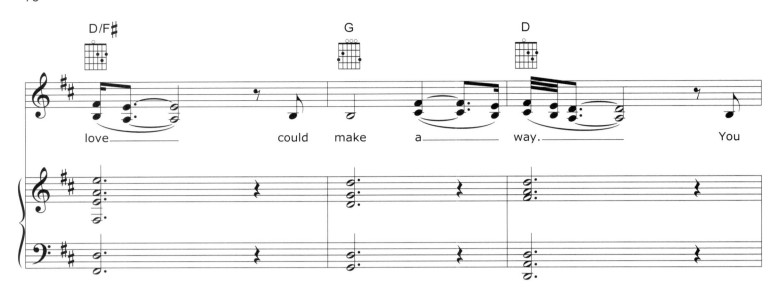

love_____ could make a_____ way._____ You

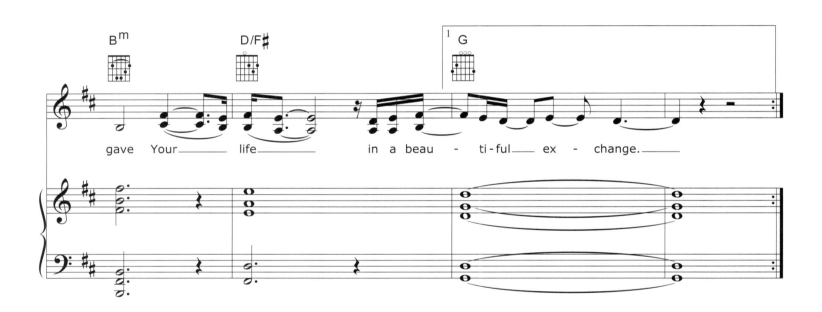

gave Your_____ life_____ in a beau - ti-ful__ ex - change._____

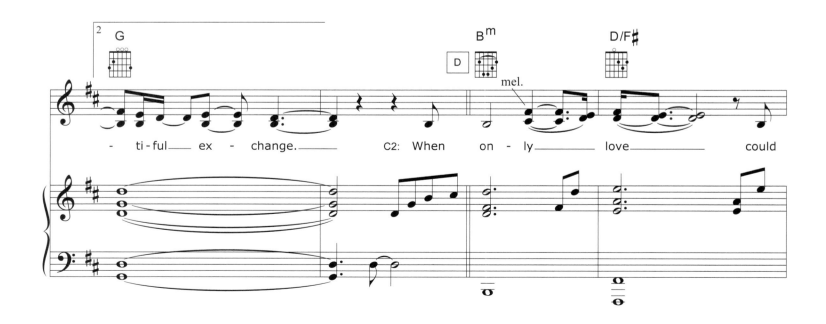

-ti-ful__ ex - change._____ C2: When on - ly__ love_____ could

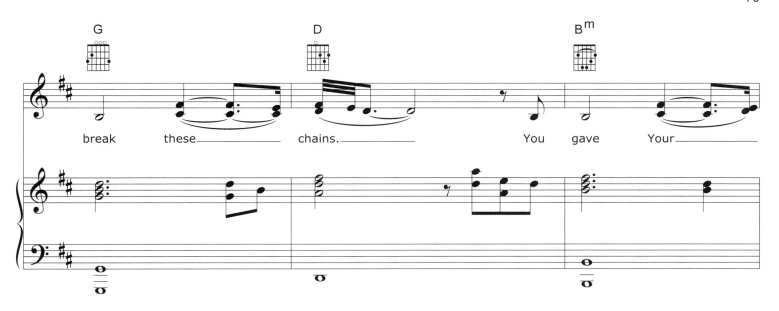

break these_____ chains._____ You gave Your_____

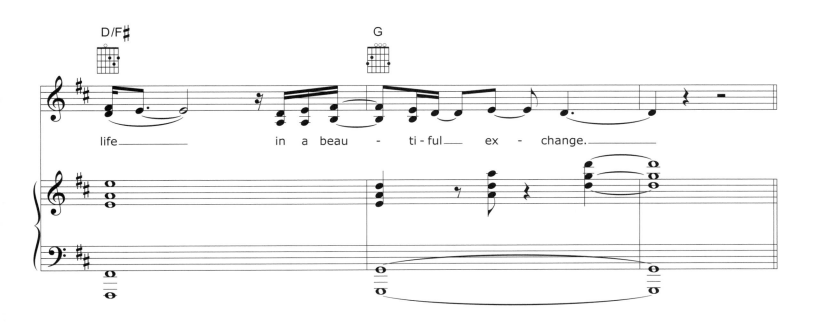

life_____ in a beau - ti - ful_____ ex - change._____

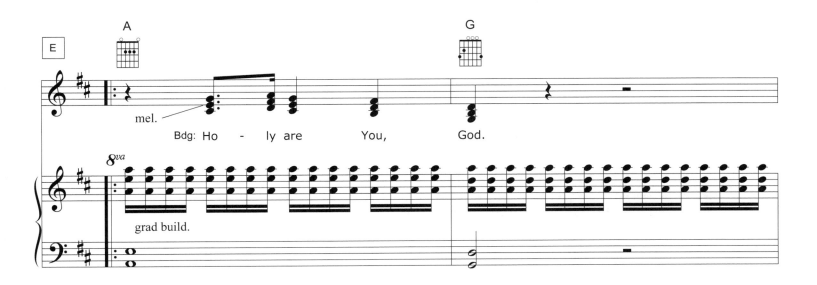

mel.

Bdg: Ho - ly are You, God.

8va

grad build.

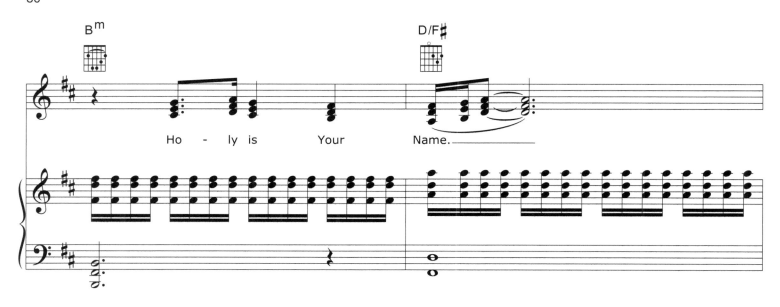

Ho - ly is Your Name.

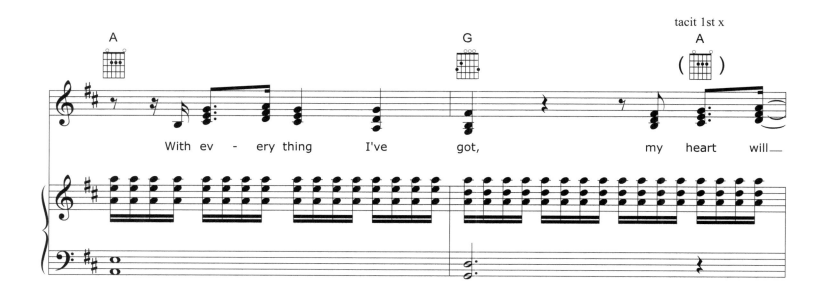

tacit 1st x

With ev - ery thing I've got, my heart will

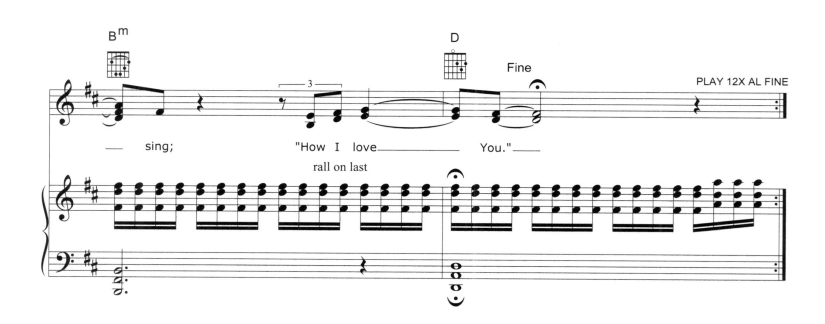

PLAY 12X AL FINE

Fine

— sing; "How I love You."

rall on last

Thank You

Words and Music by REUBEN MORGAN
and BEN FIELDING

V1: Thank You for Your kind - ness.   Thank You for Your mer - cy.

CCLI: 5637487

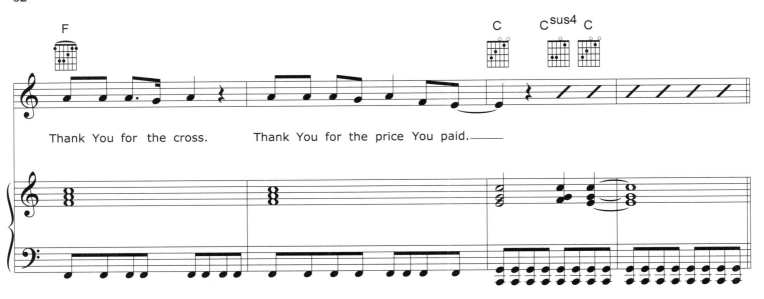

Thank You for the cross. Thank You for the price You paid.____

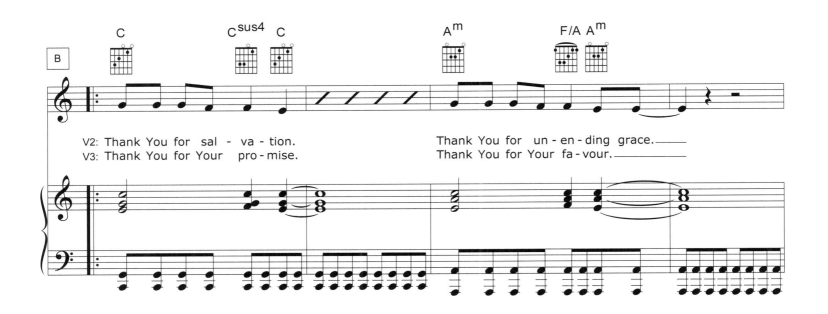

V2: Thank You for sal - va - tion.
V3: Thank You for Your pro - mise.

Thank You for un - en - ding grace.____
Thank You for Your fa - vour.____

Thank You for Your hope. Thank You for this life You give.____
Thank You for Your love, ev - ery-thing You've done for me.____

P'Chs: There is

84

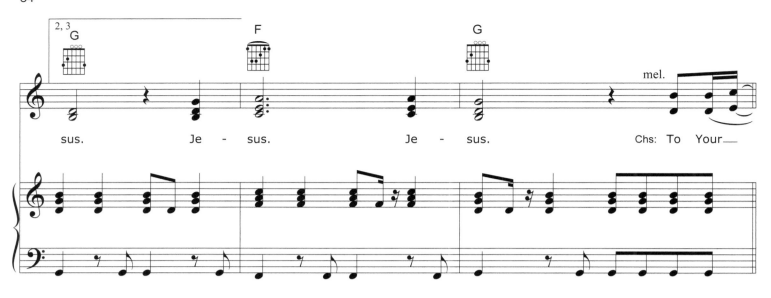